Mindfulness for Beginners

A Beginner's Guide to a Peaceful, Stress-Free, Pain-Free Life Every Day

by
Julie Simons

Published by Lindmaur Publishing

First Printing, 2013

ISBN-13: 978-0992088712

ISBN-10: 0992088712

Printed in the United States of America

Your Special Bonus!

for more Mindfulness tips

go to

http://www.bonuses4you.com/mindfulnessforbeginners

Table of Contents

Mindfulness: A Guide to Improving Your Quality of Life

Tell me, have these things ever happened to you?

- You search for your misplaced car keys, only to find them stashed in your bag or in your bedside drawer?
- You take your first sip of coffee in the morning and a minute later, notice you have only one drop left?
- You drive off to work and remember almost nothing about the trip?

In a society where every minute counts, where we seem to need to squeeze in as many obligations as our bodies can accommodate, it's easy to get lost in the hecticness of our own lives. When that alarm goes off in the morning, many of us go into auto-pilot mode and go about our day-to-day routine mindlessly, rushing from one activity to the next, often missing out on the important details that are happening in the moment. As we grapple to fulfill work demands, household chores, family and financial obligations, we lose our sense of awareness and fail to hear what our inner voice is telling us.

We human beings have developed a habit of overanalyzing the past and the future so much so that we lose sight of the present. While it may seem counterintuitive, it is only when we inculcate a deep sense of mindfulness of our feelings and thoughts without judgment that we can better create the future that lies ahead of us.

Mindfulness Defined

The principles of mindfulness go beyond simply seeing situations as they occur. Renowned mindfulness expert Jon Kabat-Zinn defines mindfulness as "a way of connecting with your life, of paying attention on purpose in the present moment non-judgmentally, as if your life depended on it." This statement is further backed by coach and therapist Dr. Patrizia Collard, who stresses the importance of mindfulness as a "wonderful tool to teach people to actually be right here, right now; not only to be right here, right now, but to accept that you're right here, right here now."

If you find Dr. Collard's statement confusing, think of it this way. Mindfulness is not about what you are focusing on, but the act of paying attention itself that matters more. When we are being attentive, we are able to vividly view situations in our lives. It helps us to take a step back and to consciously respond to present situations with a non-judgmental stance. It helps us to avoid being consumed with unnecessary worries, and to gain better insight. Only when we are mindful can we actually be present in all facets of our life, including relationships, work, and family life.

What Mindfulness Entails

Mindfulness requires constant practice. Often this practice entails special meditation exercises that help your brain have better control of how it responds to sensations, thoughts, or feelings.

Our minds don't stop for a minute. Thoughts constantly come and go. This is completely normal; it is the nature of the human brain. But it is how we react to these that matters. When we practice mindfulness, the more we are able to avoid distractions, stop being on auto-pilot, and start responding in a positive, more constructive way.

This can be achieved through what experts call the mindfulness ABC.

A is for Awareness

Awareness involves acknowledging a thought, feeling or sensation; being in the now - fully cognizant of your body, mind and emotions.

B is for Being One with the Moment

If "being one with the moment" sounds a little airy-fairy to you, think of it as shutting down distractions – thoughts, habits, and unnecessary cognitive and emotional indulgences – and simply focusing on the here and now – right now!

C is for Clarity

This means seeing things as they are, not for what we would want them to be or what they could be. By separating the moment itself from our emotional reactions to it, we can have better control over our choices and respond more effectively.

How Mindfulness Can Change Your Life

Since its introduction in the West in the 70s, the concept of mindfulness has greatly changed the way individuals view their respective lives. It has also become an effective way to alleviate a variety of physical and mental challenges – pain and depression included.

Exactly how can mindfulness benefit you as an individual? Below are just some of the key advantages of practicing mindfulness.

• **It lets you slow down and reassess your responses, be they emotional, physical or mental, so you can react more effectively to varying situations.**

By instilling a sense of awareness of yourself and your surroundings, you are able to achieve better focus and can respond to situations in a more constructive manner. When we make mindfulness a practice, we are also being conscious of the moment on a big-picture level, and thus, are able to react with conscientiousness, wisdom, and acceptance.

"We spend a huge amount of time planning and worrying about the future and a huge amount of time reminiscing the past...and the present moment which is the only time that we're ever alive in; the only time we could learn anything...is now. And yet the present moment gets completely squeezed out by all of our preoccupations in the future or in the past. When we start to pay attention in our mind and our own body, it's like reclaiming your life," Kabat-Zinn explains.

- **It allows you to perceive situations more vividly, without prior biases or criticisms.**

Meditation, a key practice in mindfulness, improves your ability to focus on situations by enhancing activity in the part of the brain that's responsible for feelings and pain.

- **It decreases stress levels and makes you more resilient.**

When we practice mindfulness, we become calm and less stressed. Cortisol, a stress hormone, also decreases, as documented in a study published in the journal Health Psychology in March 2013.

- **It boosts creativity.**

Creativity is related to the stress response. Dr. Collard notes that when we are under stress, the stress chemical released by the brain negatively impacts the part of the brain that's responsible for creativity: the frontal lobe. Studies show that mindfulness techniques improve frontal lobe activity and musical focus, as per the journal Psychology of Music.

- **It improves sleep and lessens anxiety and depression.**

According to Kabat-Zinn, in our society we were trained so much in thought but little in awareness. So when retiring to bed, many of us are unable to shut down our thoughts or deal with them constructively. "These thoughts", he said, "are only thoughts, but we believe them to be truths that pretty soon we end up sleepless, with chronic anxiety, or even depression."

Mindfulness techniques help individuals to better manage stress and anxiety, sleep better at night, as a research study at the University of Utah showed.

- **It makes you more flexible and your life, well-balanced.**

All in all, when you have improved focus and control of your thoughts and emotions, are less stressed and have better sleep, it reflects in the way you live your life. It becomes the default. You become more compassionate and reasonable, and your life is in better shape. It certainly affects those you interact with.

Mastering Meditation for Mindfulness

"Meditation brings wisdom; lack of meditation brings ignorance." – Buddha

One of the most popular and most effective techniques to develop mindfulness is to meditate. This practice has been around for centuries, and was utilized by Zen proponents in the east, including Buddha himself.

By regularly meditating, you will gain more focus and awareness and become calmer and more in tune with your mind and body.

However, hindrances may occur along the way, and by recognizing them, you will learn how to deal with them effectively.

10 Common Meditation Problems Beginners Encounter and How to Manage Them

- **Meditating when tense or stressed**

To avoid frustration, don't push yourself to meditate when you're stressed, angry, or weary. Unless you can immediately switch off that feeling (and who can?), rest first or listen to soothing music before you attempt to meditate.

- **Noise and other distractions**

Prior to meditation, always make sure that you're in a quiet spot, away from loud music, voices and other distractions. Put your phone on silent mode – yes, really! Make sure that the room temperature is neither too hot nor too cold – and to prevent sleepiness, don't eat anything before your meditation session.

- **Discomfort**

Being still for long stretches of time can be incredibly straining on the muscles, so make sure that you are in a comfortable position before meditating. Relaxed positions like sitting are advisable for beginners. The idea is simply to have as little movement as possible during the session. Pillows, back supports, and blankets can also be helpful in minimizing discomfort. (I get dizzy easily when sitting with my eyes shut, so I prefer to sit against a wall or lie down.)

- **Pushing yourself to meditate for extended periods**

Remember: This is not a contest. Aim for a quality meditation session, not necessarily a long one. Begin with a short session as you slowly begin to get the hang of it. Then increase the duration gradually over time.

- **Pressuring yourself**

Meditation requires a great deal of concentration and motivation, and pressure will not help you achieve that. Avoid getting yourself tied up in knots with "this isn't working!" Ease up and make sure you're relaxed. If you can't relax, take a few slow deep breaths. Alternatively, try again later.

- **Wrong posture**

Assuming an uncomfortable or improper position promotes strain and distraction. There are several meditative positions that can help you maintain stability and a relaxed posture. It is totally up to you to find a position that you can be comfortable in (more about postures later). Once you've gotten to the stage where you're into a longer meditation, be sure to do a slow stretch at the 15- to 30-minute mark to help with circulation.

- **Sleepiness**

Minimize sleepiness by opting to meditate at a time of day when you are particularly alert, preferably in the morning after a good sleep and an invigorating shower. Washing your face with cold water beforehand will also help.

- **Restlessness or tension**

This commonly occurs to beginners as your body is trying to shed old habits and acquaint itself with new ones, and so a new kind of energy is liberated. This is only temporary. Release tension by doing breathing exercises, walking, or running.

- **Impatience and an inability to focus**

It is common for beginners to have difficulty concentrating and to experience mental resistance. It will not help to respond with anger, disappointment, or hopelessness as this will only increase your tension and stress. Instead, acknowledge the thought, and then slowly let it go. Breathe in and out, do a few fist-clenching exercises, then slowly bring your focus back to your practice.

- **Lack of time**

Finding time to meditate is both a matter of habit and time. It takes commitment to allot even just five minutes of your time every day to meditate. Write down the reasons why you want to meditate and why it is important for you to do so. When you make that 5-minute exercise a habit, it will soon become a norm for you.

Benefits of Good Meditative Positions

We mentioned that proper posture plays a key role in lessening distractions. Adopting a proper meditative posture ensures:

- You stay awake and alert throughout the session
- You are in the best position for proper as well as easier breathing
- Your back and muscles don't get strained
- You have fewer distractions, including uninvited thoughts

- You stay relaxed and focused, providing yourself with better concentration and awareness of what you are doing

How to Begin Meditation

1. Find a quiet spot where you can comfortably assume a meditative position.
2. Find a position that can provide you with the utmost ease, comfort, and presence of mind for the duration of the practice. Movement creates distraction. Adjust your position, if necessary, but do it slowly. Your goal is to minimize movement as much as possible. (The next section provides you with recommended positions for beginners.)
3. Relax your hands. You may simply fold or rest it on your lap or knees, or have one palm on top of the other. The objective is to be aware of your hands in its position, not the kind of position.
4. While many intermediate and advanced meditators can practice meditation with open eyes, beginners are advised to shut their eyes during the process. If you choose the former, relax and lead your gaze onto the floor at a 3 to 4-feet distance. The specific choice of

object to focus on doesn't matter; it is the awareness of having your eyes rest on something that counts.

5. Make sure that your head, neck, shoulders and spine are in proper alignment. This is essential in establishing stability and duration and improving concentration.
6. Quiet your mind and free it of all thought. Listen to the silence and let mindfulness flow.

Meditative Positions for Beginners

- **Full lotus**

This is a popular position that derives from the shape of the lotus plant, which is considered sacred in Zen. It involves crossing your legs and placing either foot on the opposite thigh.

The lotus position promotes proper posture by:

- Opening the hips
- Flexing the entire leg down to the ankle
- Straightening the spine vertically

While popular, this is not an advisable position if you have leg and hip conditions (due to its degree of difficulty).

- **Half-lotus**

The half-lotus, a variation on the lotus position, involves resting one foot on the opposite thigh while the other foot rests beneath the other thigh. It has benefits that are similar to the lotus position, but is less complex and easier when you're a beginner.

- **Burmese**

The Burmese position involves resting both legs on the floor or with one in front of the other (with bent knees). The feet are not on top of the thighs. This is an easier position for balance and symmetry and less likely to cause strain or discomfort, and is also recommended if you're less flexible.

- **Kneeling position (Seiza)**

The Seiza requires you to bend your knees and place them apart at shoulder-width, with your heels, a pillow or a cushion supporting the buttocks. This position directs most of the circulation to the lower part of the body, thus allowing the upper body, particularly the head and shoulders, to be calmer, more relaxed, and more focused. Seiza is perfect if you have less hip flexibility as it is fairly easy to do and get out of.

The pose in the photo is the starting position. Begin with this position and then sit back on your heels or on a pillow.

- **Sitting**

The sitting position is perhaps the easiest position for beginners. It is done primarily for practical reasons and comfort.

Use a chair to ensure better alignment. Relax your back but keep it straight. If possible, avoid leaning back against the chair, so that your body becomes self-supporting. Your head must be erect with your chin slightly dropped. Your feet should be flat on the floor, apart at shoulder-width, just below the knees. Place your hands in your lap.

- **Lying down**

If you can't seem to find comfort in any of these positions, try lying down (but also try not to fall asleep.) To prevent lower back pain, put a rolled up towel under your knees. Here's where keeping your eyes open and focused on a spot on the ceiling throughout the meditation is a good idea!

Remember that there's no single position that suits everyone. Experiment with these positions and choose one that gives you the greatest amount of stability and concentration.

Making Mindfulness Work for You

There are other ways to achieve mindfulness in addition to meditation. In this section, we'll discuss how mindfulness and its obstacles play out day-to-day. You'll also learn some techniques to help you overcome them.

"All human beings are born with it...at some point we were all mindful – and partially due to the way our lives have speeded up, we have lost the ability to be mindful," relates psychotherapist Dr. Patrizia Collard.

It is therefore possible to return to that mindful state you were born to. There are simple mindfulness exercises and techniques you can practice to help you improve focus, concentration, and awareness of the present.

Most Common Obstacles to Being Mindful

Before we discuss these additional mindfulness techniques, it is important that you recognize the common lapses in mindfulness that happen regularly. This awareness is the first step in moving toward a more peaceful, stress-free, pain-free life. Watch out for these – and when you notice yourself lapsing into these states, make a conscious effort to stop yourself.

1. Dwelling too much in the past and overanalyzing the future

Often, we are too preoccupied with the mistakes we have made in the past - what we could've done better, why a certain situation happened the way it did, or why it did not happen the way we wanted it to - or we tend to over-anticipate and work too hard for the future that we forget about living in the Now. While both the past and the future are important in achieving a purposeful life, it is in the present moment that we can learn the tools we need for a meaningful future, and make meaning of the relationships and circumstances that we have.

2. Believing that YOU are your thoughts

We are composed of the mind, body, and spirit. Yet often, we are tricked into thinking that we are only as good as our thoughts. This not only limits our abilities, our self-confidence, and our self-esteem, but our purpose as individuals as well. Only when we recognize our dynamic nature as a person with flesh, soul, and mind can we have total control of our present, and ultimately, our lives.

3. Never taking the time to be quiet

In our society, we were trained to be communicators and that practice has turned us into talking machines that constantly entertain whatever comes to mind. What we don't realize is that when we're always talking, in reality we are never actually in tune with what other people have to say or to what our inner voice is telling us. So in essence, we don't get an opportunity to have any real relationships, even with ourselves.

4. Overly criticizing yourself

We all grew up with certain standards: that of our families, of society, of our respective cultures. In our pursuit to conform to these standards, we have developed a propensity to self-criticism. We think we need to listen to and follow what others want us to be instead of listening to what our inner voices and gut feelings are telling us. We end up believing them to be the truth (Just look at the skinny models in magazines.)

Using Mindfulness Techniques to Beat Obstacles

A recurring theme in mindfulness is being aware of what you need holistically, of what is going on in the present, and being in control of your responses to those needs and situations so as to achieve a well-balanced life. Achieve better control of your thoughts and learn mindfulness with the following techniques:

- **One-minute mindfulness exercise**

As the name denotes, this exercise takes only a minute to do and you can accomplish it anytime of the day. Take note of the time and for 60 seconds, simply focus on your breathing. During that duration, your attention should be solely focused on that. If ever you find your thoughts stray, repeat from the start until you can stay fully concentrated on your breathing for an entire minute. Once mastered, you can increase the duration of the exercise.

Here are some ideas to help you figure out when and where to grab that 1 minute: when you wake up in the morning, when you get into your car and before you drive off to your destination, just before you get out of your car, just as you're sitting down to lunch, right after you use the bathroom or take a shower, and so on.

- **Deep breathing exercise**

This is a perfect alternative if you don't have the advantage of a full meditative exercise. It can be done whether you're at work, in the office, or in the car. Focus on your breathing and begin by inhaling from the stomach, then slowly exhale through the lips and the nose. Pay attention to the sound of your breathing, and feel your chest expand. This helps soothe nerves and calms you when upset.

- **Count to ten**

This is a simple exercise to attain better concentration, which is a key tenet of mindfulness. Focus on your breathing, shut your eyes then slowly count to ten. If your mind wanders off, start back at one until you are able to focus on counting to ten without distractions.

- **Take a walk**

Walking is one of the best times to reflect and appreciate the present. Instead of hurrying, walk slowly and feel your legs and the soles of your feet as they touch the ground and lift for another step. Note the sensation it brings to your feet and your legs. Then open your senses one at a time to what's around you. Observe – notice small details, such as the colors and shapes of things around you. Smell the air. Listen. Taste. Then feel how the wind brushes against your cheeks.

- **Listen to music**

Music has been proven to provide wonderful benefits to the mind and body. In fact, music is widely used as therapy for people with varying moods and ailments, e.g. depression, cancer, dementia. It works on the healthy as well – just think about how some of your favorite songs make you feel.

To increase mindfulness, you'll need to choose music with a slow, relaxed tempo, such as Classical or New Age. Focus on the rhythm and tone of the music playing and the sensation it brings. If you again have uninvited thoughts, recognize them. Then pull yourself away from them and refocus on the Now.

Choose to be mindful. Make it a commitment. It can be tough in the beginning, but when you make it a habit, mindfulness will soon become a state of being rather than a task.

Mindfulness in Summary

One of the most well-known teachings of Buddha is, "The secret of health for both mind and body is not to mourn for the past, nor to worry about the future, but to live the present moment wisely and earnestly."

This is what mindfulness is all about. It allows you to embrace all facets of your being, including your mind, body, and spirit by promoting awareness of your present rather than lingering on the past or over planning the future. By slowing down and paying attention to what is right now, you are able to perceive and respond to feelings, thoughts, and physical sensations clearly and more effectively, thereby avoiding mistakes, pain, and stress.

In a nutshell, mindfulness allows you to enjoy more freedom, take better control of your present life, and get more out of your experiences.

Living in the Now

If you live in the past or in the future, then you are living in a non-existent world. Yesterday and tomorrow are mere concepts. Yet, we spend too much time rehashing what has happened and worrying about what will happen, not knowing that doing so affects not only the way we view things, but also how our body reacts. This compulsive worrying negatively impacts our physical, emotional, psychological, and spiritual health: the brain structure and function becomes limited, stress levels and emotional baggage increase, the risk for anxiety and depression goes up, and the spirit becomes a hollow, debilitated shell - facts already proven by many clinical studies.

We function on auto-pilot as we rush from one task to the next and the next and the next. (Have you ever forgotten where you parked your car because you were so intent on getting to your destination that you didn't turn around to make note of where you left it?) We never stop to observe and to listen; our responses and behavior are clouded by a certain mindlessness. This not only results in mishaps at times, but also in missing the point of ever living at all. The present moment is really the only time when you can ever learn and develop relationships with yourself, as well as with everyone and everything around you. The Now is when the real stuff is happening.

Start Living Today: Incorporating 7 Mindfulness Techniques Into Your Life

How do we start living in the present? We start by being mindful of the simplest things. Incorporate mindfulness in your daily living through:

- **Mindful eating**

Don't just gobble your food down – and don't eat while reading or watching TV. Slow down and take the time to taste the diverse flavors of food in your mouth; how the textures play in your tongue; how that glass of wine smells before you take a sip. Listen to your tummy when it says it is full.

- **Mindful meditating**

Meditating can do wonders for the mind, body and spirit. It enhances concentration. In meditation, it is not the object that you are focusing on that matters, it is the awareness of the act of concentrating on something. Go back and implement the various techniques and positions to achieve successful meditation that you've read about in this book.

- **Mindful listening**

Listen with intent. Play soothing music and notice the vibration, rhythm, tone, tempo and sensation it brings. When speaking with others, don't cut them off because you're eager to have your say. Listen to the words and to the intent and feelings behind those words.

- **Mindful talking**

Think before you talk. Listen intently to the person talking and to yourself before responding. Sometimes, you don't even need to speak. Silence speaks volumes.

- **Mindful thinking**

Don't pass judge on to the present situation. Simply witness life and listen to your thoughts as they unfold.

- **Mindful walking**

Walking is one of the easiest and most refreshing ways to be aware of your body because it involves all senses. It offers personal space to reflect on how every part of your body and mind is reacting to sensations. The next time you take a walk, do it hastily. Take the time to notice the way your feet touches the ground; how the wind feels; listen to the sounds; see the sights. Do it all without judgment.

- **Mindful breathing**

Pay attention to your breathing. Notice how the chest expands and constricts. When you are stressed, angry or frustrated, breathe. Inhale from the belly; then slowly exhale into the mouth and the nose. Do this until the negative emotion subsides.

Easy Mindfulness Acronyms to Keep You on Track

There are a couple of helpful acronyms that we mindfulness-loving folks use as tools to remind ourselves to concentrate and focus.

The first is **RAIN**.

Recognizing what's happening in the present (emotion, situation, etc.)

Allowing life to unfold as is -- acknowledging events, thoughts, and others without judgment

Investigating the inner experience – paying attention to your thoughts and emotions

Non-identifying – witness what's happening without identifying it as permanent

The second acronym is **STOP**.

Stop what you're doing

Take a breather

Observe your feelings, thoughts, and sensations

Proceed with those things that can provide you with support, like music or family

While mindfulness takes its roots from Buddhist and Zen theologies, mindfulness itself is not a religion, and can be enjoyed by people from all walks of life, young or old, regardless of their religious beliefs. Make mindfulness a habit, a part of your lifestyle – whether you're doing the chores or going to the office. Live in the moment. Choose to be aware. Only when you do so can you live purposefully and without regret.

About the Author

Julie Simons has been a practicing life coach for the past 15 years.

She has a natural inclination to help others succeed and has found that incorporating mindfulness practice into her coaching sessions has helped her clients increase their focus, concentration, and mental clarity. As a result, Julie has witnessed their increased personal fulfillment, achievement, and success in reaching their goals.

In ***Mindfulness for Beginners: A Beginner's Guide to a Peaceful, Stressful, Pain-Free Life Every Day***, she aims to help others learn to incorporate mindfulness into their lives so they too can reap the benefits.

Bonus Report

Quick reminder:

in case you missed the bonus offer at the beginning of this book, go to

http://www.bonuses4you.com/mindfulnessforbeginners

for your special report

4202296R00025

Printed in Great Britain
by Amazon.co.uk, Ltd.,
Marston Gate.